PRAISE FOR THE WRITING OF
ROBERT JOHN EMMONS

"*Six Thousand Sunrises*…The title fires the imagination. For the first time in human history, millions have the opportunity and challenge of yet another creative period in their lives, a time hitherto mostly devoted to exiting and not new beginnings. This book is an important journey, for Robert Emmons and, more importantly, for the reader as well."

–Ronald V. Gallo, EdD
CEO Santa Barbara Foundation

"Robert Emmons sees beyond the superficial aspects of experience to the realities at the center of our lives."

–N. Scott Momaday
Pulitzer Prize-winning novelist and poet

"Robert Emmons' passion for life is the basis for all his poems, whether celebrating life's pleasures or mourning lives squandered and lost. His poems are an invitation to visit new heights."

–Chryss Yost
Coeditor *California Poetry*

"Robert Emmons has written a beautiful book that combines the perspective of a life well lived with a call to continued deep engagement with all that life brings. His message is both timeless and timely, calling us to embrace each new day as an opportunity to expand the great vistas of life by living fully in the moment. *Six Thousand Sunrises* is filled with wisdom and insight."

–Gayle Beebe, PhD
President, Westmont College

D1554349

Books by Robert John Emmons

The American Franchise Revolution
The American Franchise Revolution—Japan
Other Places, Other Times
Love and Other Minor Tragedies
The Road to Paradise
The Wanderer, a Poet's Journey
Seafarers, Poems of the Sea
Love Shadows
Six Thousand Sunrises

SIX THOUSAND SUNRISES

*Making the Most of Every Day
in Your Senior Years*

Robert John Emmons

*To Seymour
and Jane
with warm regards
and best wishes
for the holiday season.
Bob Emmons*

AMERICAN ACADEMY PRESS

An American Academy Press book
Printed in the United States

Library of Congress Control Number 2012911814

ISBN 0615663842
ISBN-13 9780615663845

First Edition

ACKNOWLEDGMENT

I am indebted to Charles Donelan for his counsel and perspective, which have influenced this book. I am also fortunate to have the continued support and insight of my trusted assistant Karen Treviño. The encouragement from family and friends is much appreciated as well, especially from my beautiful wife Christine Emmons and my children and grandchildren, who put great energy toward keeping me young in spirit.

CONTENTS

- Changes in longevity and demographics have created different patterns of living at every age.
- A new generation has come into being: post-middle age, but pre-old age.
- This emerging generation, the six thousand sunrises generation, can change the world for the good by becoming more actively self-aware.
- At the same time, extraordinary examples of lives well lived into their super senior years are all around us.

- The practical consequences of major recent demographic shifts are clear: there are more people than ever over sixty-five, and the majority of them are as physically capable and mentally acute as people fifty or younger were in previous generations.
- This new life passage, Adulthood Two, runs counter to the stereotypes about life after age sixty-five that marginalize seniors today.
- The imaginative rhetorical strategies of a CEO-turned-poet help redefine what our increased longevity can mean to us as individuals and as a society.

- Embracing the transition to a life of active wisdom means knowing when to move on and how to plan ahead.
- Passion remains the basis for accomplishment.

- It's time to reflect on the identities that your work has given you.

- You can discover new ways to meet those needs.
- You can also increase your capacity for creative thinking.
- You will find that travel is both a plan for living and a metaphor for growth.

- Communities have pressing needs; as part of the actively wise generation, you can help.
- The growth of nonprofit organizations and their changing role in contemporary society and the economy means new opportunities to give back.

- Medicine is redefining old age.
- Being physically active has multiple benefits.
- Intimacy builds a caring, sensual life.

- Educate yourself by getting to know your spouse, your children, and your grandchildren even better.
- If you can't fix your family, invent a new one.

- Enriching other lives will enrich yours more.
- Reaching out to those less fortunate can be the beginning of a new, satisfying adventure.

- A healthy, reflective attitude towards the transition from working to retirement will help you achieve a more complete senior life.
- Your sense of self-worth can improve dramatically by helping others. Accepting nonprofit leadership roles can satisfy the need for continued achievement and recognition.
- The ultimate goal is to leave this world a better place for your existence.

ABOUT THE AUTHOR

Robert John Emmons has been an entrepreneur, business doctor, and international consultant to companies around the world; and he has served as CEO of both American Stock Exchange and New York Stock Exchange companies. He has also been a university professor and is the author of an internationally published marketing book and six collections of poetry.

Emmons has served as chairman and/or trustee of numerous nonprofit organizations, including the Santa Barbara Foundation, the Mosher Foundation, the Santa Barbara Museum of Art, Lotusland Botanical Gardens, Marymount School, Laguna Blanca School, San Francisco's Philharmonia Baroque Orchestra, the Community Arts and Music Association, Loyola Marymount University, Unity Shoppe, and the International Food Industry Crusade Against Hunger. He has received the Herbert Hoover Humanitarian Award, the Los Angeles Boy Scouts of America Distinguished Citizen Award, the Food For All Humanitarian Award, the Santa Barbara News-Press Lifetime Achievement Award, the KEYT Man of the Year Award, University of Southern California's Executive of the Year Award, and the Westmont College Medal for Community Leadership.

Always opening new doors and embarking on new adventures, Emmons traveled to Italy in 2012 to take sculpture lessons at the Florence Academy of Art.

PREFACE:
A NOTE FROM THE AUTHOR

Right now I feel unusually aware of two unprecedented recent changes—one in my own life and the other in the greater world that we all share. I'll start with the global and then move to the personal. In the last decade, the world has changed more than at any time since the end of the Second World War. We seem to be living in an era in which nothing stays the same for long, and there are no guarantees.

In my life, these same years have brought unprecedented fulfillment and satisfaction on every level. My youngest child just graduated from a prestigious university—a semester early, no less—and is, at the age of twenty-one, on his way to a career as an entrepreneur. My wife and I have just experienced yet another of our shared adventures. In this episode we lived in Florence, Italy, where I studied sculpture at the Florence Academy of Art and Christine explored the city through photography.

Now none of this should shock you and neither should what I am about to say. In fact I've written this book so that the next thing I say will cease to shock anyone. Later this year, 2012, I will celebrate my eightieth birthday.

Unintentionally, I seem to have become a spokesperson for an important emerging demographic of men and women who are living well into their eighties without experiencing the diminished expectations usually associated with old age. I strongly believe that aging doesn't have to mean growing old, and I want to share the good news about this discovery to everyone who plans to enjoy the later years of life.

I can't explain how to live this longer, better life with just a few simple instructions; I'm going to have to use some poetry. My life as a writer began with poetry, and I remain convinced that metaphors matter. In the search for meaning in life, figures of speech will always play a role—and with good reason—because we could not share what we think and feel without them. And thinking and feeling are what the good life is all about.

Strangely enough, I found the metaphor I needed for my poetic description of the senior years in the actuarial tables. According to the Prudential Insurance Company, today's average sixty-five-year-old retiree can look forward to *six thousand sunrises* before reaching the age of life expectancy: eighty-three. The current life-expectancy figure of eighty-three is a fairly prosaic fact; those sunrises, on the other hand, are poetry. They expanded to fill my imagination, and they helped me crystallize years of thinking and feeling about growing better as you grow older into the book you are holding now.

In a way, the difference between the abstract facts of our lives and the meaningful poetry within them is the real point of this book. Our increasing collective longevity is one thing in the abstract, but it's quite another when you imagine those eighteen years in terms of their six thousand potential sunrises.

That's six thousand days just waiting to be filled with the light and hope of personal change, wise adaptation, and renewed purpose. We often use the expression "it dawned on me" to describe the birth of an idea; in this case, it's especially appropriate.

When I first thought about that image of six thousand sunrises, I saw the challenges and rewards of later life more completely than I ever had before. I had been going along for years just doing the things that came naturally to me: helping others, enjoying the arts, bringing people together, and savoring the company of my friends and family. But almost without noticing it, I had done these things at an age when many of my peers were demanding less rather than more out of life. They were accepting routines and attitudes that very often seemed abruptly to have shrunk.

When I finally understood this difference between my experience and that of many of my contemporaries, I wanted to share the observations I've made about how to live each day to the fullest. My goal is to spread the word that you can have an extraordinary life in your senior years, that you can still achieve impressive results through concerted effort, and that you can have a lot of fun along the way.

Living each of our days to the fullest carries with it a responsibility to those we touch as we bask in the light of this special gift. In "Song of Myself," the most important poem by America's greatest poet, Walt Whitman, the speaker articulates my guiding principle, the core metaphor for my entire philosophy. "Dazzling and tremendous how quick the sun-rise would kill me," Whitman writes, "if I could not now and always send sun-rise out of me."

In one stroke, the poet's imagination takes him out of the category of life's victims—those who would let something as benign and life-affirming as the sunrise kill them—and vaults him into the universe, making of him another sun and making him capable of centering a solar system of personal power and creative potential. This concept of sending sunrise takes the metaphor of the six thousand sunrises and turns it into a practice and a process, something from which we can derive strength for the hard moments and take pleasure in the good ones. Indeed, making a place in those sunlit days for your fellow travelers, particularly those less fortunate, is a rewarding way to let your personal sunrise enrich the lives of others and add greater meaning to your journey.

So as I close out these words of explanation about why I undertook this project and what I think it can do for you, let's agree on one thing. Let's agree now that together we will use our talents and the ideas, examples, poems, and exercises in this book to make the most of life's daily gift. Let's agree to be the kind of sunrises that project an optimistic spirit of understanding, compassion, hope, and joy. Spend your energy on bringing light to where you find darkness, and you will succeed in sending sunrise out of yourself to those you meet as you travel the paths of life.

INTRODUCTION:
A NEW PARADIGM FOR HOW TO
LIVE WELL IN YOUR SENIOR YEARS

The secret of genius is to carry the spirit
of the child into old age, which means
never losing your enthusiasm.

–Aldous Huxley

In recent years the different stages of life have received considerable attention. Each of these stages represents a different set of life issues worth recognizing. These passages have been defined in a number of ways, but here I'll refer to them as:

Early Years 1 – 39 years
Middle Age 40 – 59 years
Senior   60 – 79 years
Super Senior 80+ years

These passages haven't always been the same. As medical advances have significantly increased life expectancy and our ability to function well into the later years, seniors and super seniors have found themselves still capable of what the generation before had abandoned in middle age. There are simply more seniors around, too. According to the most recent census, ten thousand people turn sixty-five every day. Today a seventy-five-year-old man in good health can expect to live into his late eighties. As a consequence, Social Security, retirement income, medical costs, and senior care have changed, too; and many providers are under considerable stress. A much greater focus on retirement planning, including extending the working years, might help; but in general, we all need to take these changes into consideration.

Financial institutions have recognized this new reality as well. Wells Fargo Bank, which helps many people with their retirement planning, recently proclaimed that eighty is the new sixty-five. The bank has noticed that many people are delaying retirement to build a retirement war chest. Delaying retirement will also result in increased Social Security payments when retirement eventually occurs, adding yet another strain to the system.

But this book is not about how banks and governments should deal with this new reality, but about how you should. To enjoy exciting and fulfilling senior years, you must capitalize on opportunities for life enrichment. If you maintain an inquisitive, youthful attitude, you can enjoy the benefits of what you have accomplished while exploring new avenues for enhanced self-worth.

Remember, life is like a parade; too many people simply watch it go by. Don't just stand there on the corner! Experience as much as you can, and don't pass up the opportunity to have a positive impact on the lives of others. Truly helping someone, such as providing a scholarship to a good student and then watching him graduate from college, is an exhilarating experience that gives you a great wellspring of psychic rewards.

Let's take a look at some special people who have navigated the super senior years with considerable success. Each has been willing to explore different careers and, in some cases, different lifestyles. Each was willing to take risks that opened new doors to personal fulfillment. They all reinvented themselves periodically as interesting opportunities came up. They changed their lives from time to time, and they were enriched by the process.

For instance, take a look at one of my favorite people, Jack Nadel. He is eighty-eight years old and recently published his fifth book. He and his step-daughter maintain a website called http://www.jack-nadel.com, which focuses on his experience as an entrepreneur who operated successfully in Europe, Asia, and the United States. While Jack has had to deal with some of the infirmities that often come with his age, his spirit is youthful, his mind is quick, and he is full of fresh ideas. His television program, *Out of the Box,* has had an impressive guest list of entrepreneurs and become a staple for viewers in California. Jack has also focused on music and healthcare in his extensive philanthropy.

Jack isn't the only super senior on my list. The sculptor Aris Demetrios, now enjoying his eightieth year, still produces modern monumental sculptures that adorn public spaces across the United States and internationally from Asia to the Middle East. You can see his work at the University of California Merced, University of Southern California, Santa Barbara City College, and Stanford University, among many other places. Right now, he's writing a memoir that chronicles his life as the son of Virginia Burton, the children's book author and icon, and George Demetrios, the sculptor. Aris will also introduce three major monumental works of sculpture in 2012. He has served as mentor to a large group of young sculptors starting their professional careers.

Another extraordinarily active super senior, Lady Leslie Ridley-Tree is both the president of an international airplane parts distributor in Santa Monica, California, and one of the most generous philanthropists in Santa Barbara, California. She has funded major projects at the Santa Barbara Zoo, Santa Barbara Museum of Art, the Casa Esperanza community kitchen, Cottage Hospital, and Westmont College, among others. She has also found time to serve on the boards of nearly a dozen of Santa Barbara's nonprofit organizations. Early in her life, Lady Leslie was a social worker in New York, a nightclub singer, and a paralegal for a prominent Los Angeles law firm. She is an avid art collector, music patron, and world traveler.

Barnaby Conrad, another good friend, has reinvented himself numerous times in his eighty-nine years. He is a successful artist and author who had a distinguished diplomatic career as well, serving as a US State Department vice consulate in Spain from 1943 to 1946.

Barnaby attended the School of Fine Arts at the University of Mexico and is a graduate of the School of Fine Arts at Yale University. As recently as 2005, he held an exhibit of his paintings in Santa Barbara.

Having worked as a secretary to famed novelist Sinclair Lewis early in his writing career, Barnaby has published thirty-five books of both fiction and nonfiction. His most recent novel, *The Second Life of John Wilkes Booth,* was published in 2010. He has fought bulls in Spain, Mexico, and Peru; and his novel *Matador* sold nearly two million copies in twenty languages. His nightclub, El Matador, was the center of artistic life in San Francisco for a number of years and the place where Herb Caen, Pulitzer Prize-winning columnist and *San Francisco Chronicle* icon, held court every Wednesday afternoon.

Barnaby founded the Santa Barbara Writers Conference in 1973, leading it and mentoring numerous young authors until he retired in 2004. He is currently working on a collection of short stories.

Charcoal portrait of Robert John Emmons
by Barnaby Conrad

All four of these octogenarians have filled their lives to the fullest and represent what we would all like to experience. We can learn from their stories. The key is to pursue what moves you, what interests you, and what gratifies you.

The lesson you can learn from these lives well lived is that there are opportunities to enlarge and enrich other people's lives without necessarily making major course changes in your own life. What it takes to live lives like these is generally optimism and positive thinking. These wonderful people are the forebears for a new generation of seniors whose credo is, "Yes, I can!" not "No, I can't."

The power of optimism is indeed incredible. Your attitude can deliver extraordinary results. Your optimism can stimulate those around you to think more positively. This kind of positive thinking can raise everyone's spirits. For instance, a new Internet clothing company started in 2012 by merely using the phrase, "I Feel Great" (http://www.ifeelgreatclothing.com). When people see this emblazoned on clothing, it lifts their spirits as they share this optimistic message. The mirror effect can return to you the sunrises you send to others. When you face your days with a positive outlook and a can-do attitude, you would be amazed at what you can accomplish.

With every new sunrise comes the opportunity to make a difference in the lives of others. You can help someone who lives in terrible circumstances embrace hope and change things for the better. Philanthropy, whether in terms of money or personal assistance, can introduce the possibility of a brighter tomorrow to one who despairs. We are doubly enriched in the process. As we journey through the remainder of this book, we will explore this issue even more.

PLEASE WRITE IN THIS BOOK! Consider it your workbook and resource for planning those six thousand sunrises.

winter promise

the snow began at midnight
falling on your shining face
whitening your hair
as you walked
bent to the wind
transforming you
into an old woman

your beauty still shines,
an image, a glimpse
of years to come

it makes me smile
i want to grow old
with you at my side
to walk the years away
through many snows
to have your shining face
warm my frosty years

CHAPTER 1
THE VOYAGE NEVER ENDS

Go confidently in the direction of your dreams.
Live the life you have imagined.
–Henry David Thoreau

If you think of life as a never-ending voyage, it can significantly change your perspective. Think of your different jobs as ports that you visit. Sometimes you stay there awhile; but then the sea beckons and you set off again, seeking another beautiful sunrise in another place.

Seeing life this way challenges those of us who have devoted many years to a single organization, losing sight of all that we might have done or been if we had only moved on. It's not too late to discover some of those other possibilities if you change your thinking.

At the end of this chapter, I'll give you two lists that will help you overcome your reservations and embark once again on your never-ending voyage. One is a list of *No, I can't!* reasons for staying where you are, the other a list of *Yes, I can!* thoughts that will help you set sail. But first I should tell you about why you should change and why I wrote this book.

Let me start with a broad observation: most people identify closely with the company or organization they serve. Often the first question we ask anyone we have just met is, "What do you do?" Just as frequently the answer comes back with two pieces of information: (1) the speaker's professional identity, as in "I'm an account executive" or "I'm a lion tamer," and (2) the name of an organization that validates that identity, as in "...with First National Trust Bank" or "...with Ringling Brothers." These two pieces of information often reflect the speaker's sense of self-worth. If you hear someone say, "I am a vice president of IBM," you hear more than the name of a profession and a place of work. You also hear something about who this person really *is*.

This sense of self-identity has a long history. In the past, many people devoted their entire lives to working for a single company and considered their final job title at the company a sign of lifelong achievement.

Although this kind of career is far less common today, stable employment—and stable income—is still one of the most valued aspects of a successful career. This kind of stability can represent a problem, however, for people whose devotion to their company comes to dominate their lives.

Commitment is a wonderful thing, but each of us needs a life much larger than a single organization, no matter how large, can hold. In addition to stability and security, we all need a life that takes advantage of the opportunities the six thousand sunrises can offer. Work is important, but thinking about life in larger terms can be much more fulfilling.

This realization may come as a surprise to those of you who have spent a lifetime building a professional identity and devoting your time and energy to work. But as we move through middle age and approach our senior years, even the most career-minded among us begin to ask ourselves questions such as, "Who would I like to be? How do I replace work in a work-dominated life? What might I find rewarding? What might promote achievement, provide recognition, and enhance my sense of self-worth?" A few of the happiest people I know not only asked themselves these questions but found the answers.

For instance, many of my friends in the business world have gone on to second careers in other fields, especially teaching. I know a nuclear engineer who worked at General Electric. He retired, built a woodworking shop in his garage, and became a furniture maker. Not long after that, he became a professor at a community college. Another friend, a successful businesswoman from Maine, has devoted her retirement years to becoming an artist and teaching at an art school. Another retired businessperson, a corporate executive, now teaches computer skills to other retirees at the senior center and to third graders at the local parochial school.

Teachers get to change, too. I know a teacher who retired after many years at the same elementary school and now works almost full-time at her former part-time job as a volunteer at the local hospital. She also takes courses at the community college toward becoming a watercolor painter.

All of these success stories contain one essential element: a fulfilling substitute for work. All of these people have found something to do that enables them to redefine themselves and enrich their lives.

Of course it's not always that easy. The biggest difficulty is taking the first step because traveling to a new place in your life requires risk-taking, and few people take risks without encouragement and some expectation of a reward. That first step also requires a new way of thinking, so that's where we will begin.

First it's worth remembering that you have to abandon a lot of comfortable thoughts to get yourself going. Conventional thinking—staying within the lines of well-established ideas and beliefs—always favors the status quo, leaving us with rigid boxes of stereotypical assumptions about various people and groups. These disabling preconceptions are especially prevalent in older people who have accumulated stereotypes over a lifetime.

However difficult it might be, you must overcome these stereotypes because they prevent you from exploring new possibilities. Stereotypes tell you a terrible lie. They say, "What you are today is what you will be for the rest of your life, and there's nothing you can do to change who you are." Another lie follows the first one: "Life is preordained, so why take a risk?" When you listen to these lies, you fail to take the risks that can open the door to new beginnings and dramatically enrich your life.

But if those are the lies, then what's the truth? The truth is, do almost anything—just take action. Leonardo da Vinci, the great artist, inventor, and creative thinker, said, "Inaction saps the vigor of the mind." Most of us make excuses for inaction. There are always reasons for standing still with one's life. Wayne Dyer, the famous psychologist, says the first step in inventing the new you is to eliminate those excuses. Just imagine how expansive your life might become if you were to experience the freedom of thrusting aside the excuses that stand in the way.

So take a risk. Try something new and different. Get ready for the big leap by beginning to experiment while you are still working at your regular job. Don't think of retirement as the end; think of it as a beginning. Not much new will happen if you envision life after you retire as just a lot of sitting around. Instead, if you think of senior life as a voyage to new lands filled with promise, excitement, and discovery, you will cast yourself in the role of an explorer with a great appetite for things new and different. Your story isn't ending. You're simply starting a new chapter.

The idea of starting new adventures this late in life can be daunting, even frightening, but embarking on a new adventure during our senior years is truly stimulating. I worried a lot about my decision to attend the Florence Academy of Art in Italy to study sculpting. I didn't know whether I was up to the task either physically or emotionally. But I persevered and discovered something amazing from this new and challenging experience: if you accept the challenge, the energy will come.

Escaping your comfort zone will make you more confident, smarter, happier, more grateful, and more satisfied with life while strengthening ties to the people you care about.

The world of science even has concrete evidence of our untapped capacity for new challenges. Anthropologist Mary Catherine Bateson speaks authoritatively about how seniors are taking advantage of medical advances and finding extraordinary energy at remarkably advanced ages. "Biomedicine has once again created a profound change in the human condition," she says. "We have inserted a new developmental state into the life cycle, a second stage of adulthood, not an extension tacked onto old age."

Bateson goes on to say that seniors today have an unprecedented level of health, energy, time, and resources that allows them to fit into society in new ways, much like younger adults. This can be defined as a new age of active wisdom for those of advanced years or, in other words, *Adulthood Two*.

But taking part in this exciting new stage of life requires more than risk-taking. You must learn to keep adapting to new circumstances. When the world around you is changing dramatically, clinging to the past—particularly when you have little control over the circumstances—is counterproductive. With these expanded resources and extended life cycle, the future is seemingly without limitations, but only if you are ready to change.

Great works of literature have shown us the consequences of failing to adapt. For instance, the great Italian novel *The Leopard* by Giuseppe Tomasi di Lampedusa gives us a tragic figure. In the novel, the prince of Salina, whose family held the title for generations, clings to the old world of noble privilege even when Garibaldi's revolution has united Italy and left the world of the Italian nobility behind forever. As the prince watches his nephew join Garibaldi and embrace the new world, the prince becomes overwhelmed. He is asked to take on the role of a senator in the newly formed democratic government but declines, only to see the mayor, a buffoon, accept the position. The prince's opportunity to become part of the new world is lost forever, and he must watch helplessly as a much lesser man receives the honor.

Like the prince of Salina, many people approaching retirement today face a world changing so fast they hardly recognize it. If they cling to the past, they stay frozen in time and watch their world shrink around them. Think of the people you know who just couldn't manage one more transformation of their world. They now spend their time wishing it were still 1980 or 1950. Time doesn't stand still or go backward no matter how much you might wish it would.

But you don't have to stay frozen in time if you don't want to. Be a change realist instead. Accept the fact that change is the reality of life in the twenty-first century. Don't fight it. Accept and embrace it. Add new ports to your life's voyage; celebrate each new and exciting experience. Start by reading this list and moving from "No, I can't!" to "Yes, I can!"

OVERCOMING BARRIERS TO CHANGE

NO, I CAN'T!	YES, I CAN!
1. I have family responsibilities.	Involve your family in the process of change. Show the positive side of what you are proposing and how it might benefit the family.
2. I have a full-time job.	Use your spare time and weekends to research how you might facilitate the change with a plan and a timetable.
3. I never graduated from college.	Community college evening programs can carry you through an AA degree, and state colleges offer evening bachelor's degree programs. Internet courses can also facilitate degree completion, including a master's.

4. I have an established career at my company.

If you love your work and are fulfilled by your job, stay there until you retire. Place your emphasis on preparing for retirement, beginning with a planning process at least five years before you retire. Include new activities and responsibilities in your plan so you will have something interesting and challenging to replace your work.

5. My spouse has a good job and can't move.

Modern couples are frequently faced with this decision. Often it comes down to which career is the most promising. The winner has to ensure that the partner making the sacrifice is appreciated and supported in his or her career change as well.

NO, I CAN'T!	YES, I CAN!
6. I am too old to make life changes of this magnitude.	God has given you a greatly expanded life cycle opportunity. If eighty is the new sixty-five and your health is good, your youthful mindset will carry you forward to a time of great personal fulfillment.
7. I cannot afford the risk. What if I fail?	A life well lived, including my own, has often been buffeted by failures and disappointments. Press on! You must risk to achieve anything worthwhile.

8. It will take a long time to accomplish. I don't know if I have the energy.

Old Chinese proverb: "A journey of one thousand miles begins with the first step." You have the time; your courage will sustain you.

9. It will be too difficult to accomplish. It is an impossible dream.

Think of it as a series of steps. Break your journey down to a number of stages and focus fractionally rather than on the end result.

10. I have never done anything like this before. I will have to navigate through new territory. It is frightening.

The world around you is going to change significantly. Accept it, plan for it, and do your best to stay ahead of the curve. As you build on a series of small victories, you will become more confident.

The Stuff of Dreams

Dreams take hold from
boundless imagination, from
visions of life beyond our
reach, from the unlimited
far horizons of youth,
from the self-confidence to
manage rejections and defeat,
from the all-consuming desire
to recreate one's self for the new
world of his passionate dream.

Dreams are crushed by stifling
convention and conformity,
by the unbelievers who tell
us what cannot be, by those
willing to accept mediocrity
as a life's standard, by those
who have tried and failed and
convinced themselves it was
never possible.

Wrap your arms around
your dreams, drive off
the naysayers and philistines,
embrace your new tomorrow
with the passion to make
your dreams, your truth.

CHAPTER 2
BECOMING AN AGENT OF CHANGE:
THE MIND SHIFT

The true way to render age vigorous is to
prolong the youth of the mind.
–Mortimer Collins

For many of us, work is a place of joy and excitement, with new challenges to stimulate us constantly appearing on the horizon. We feel fulfilled when collaborating with teammates on important projects. To make the transition from work to retirement successfully, you need to treat retirement as an opportunity to create the same sense of satisfaction. It's time to find new challenges and new teams, but first you have to become an agent of change.

Let me go back a bit to explain what I mean. Many years ago when I joined Smart & Final (NYSE), I discovered that many of the younger associates did not appreciate the importance of their work. To them it did not matter whether they showed up or not because they thought their roles were insignificant. Evidence of this attitude was everywhere, but it showed up most clearly in the abnormally high rate of sick days employees took during the year. This statistic made a clear statement on behalf of those employees: "If my role is not important, I need not show up every day."

Rather than punish these associates for their absenteeism, we chose to work on the cause of the problem. We decided to celebrate the importance of everyone's work in concrete, meaningful ways. We formed the I Make a Difference program that recognized the value of everyone's contribution. Soon I Make a Difference badges adorned everyone's work clothes. We gave awards to the most productive employees, recognized their efforts in the company newsletter, and also gave team awards to outstanding groups. In addition we gave employees a real stake in the success of the company through stock-purchase programs. We also helped them with their professional development by establishing Smart University, an educational unit with more than fifty business-related courses to assist all associates in keeping up with the accelerated rate of organizational change taking place in the company.

These changes transformed the workplace. Every associate's contribution became important to every other associate. One even said to me, "Now I know why I work here." As you can imagine, the use of sick days dropped dramatically and every aspect of performance improved.

I'm proud of being part of this achievement in company management, and I learned a lot about leadership from it. I realized that the challenge for every leader is, "How can I make this organization an exciting place in which to work? How can I make this a place where everyone is pleased to come to work?"

As the late Steve Jobs, cofounder and former CEO of Apple Computer, said, "The only way to do great work is to love what you do. If you haven't found it, keep looking. Don't settle." If you've been fortunate enough to find work that you love to do, you learned this great truth from experience. But how do we keep the excitement going?

Many of us reach a point in our lives when the freshness disappears, routine dominates, and every day is the same as the one before. What can you do if this happens while you're still working? You can change to a different department, take on a different role, transfer to a different region, or join a new company with dynamic leadership. There are alternatives, but as Steve Jobs said, don't settle. Take charge of your life. Put the joy and excitement back into your every day.

If you're ready to take the bigger leap and retire from your main career, you need to prepare. First make a plan for a life change. Place a priority on economic security that will open doors and give you more options. Above all avoid allowing yourself to become trapped. Go back to school, earn a master's degree, develop a new vocation, start a new business, find your artistic self. Experience that dramatic mind shift from the shackles of the past to the incredible possibilities of the future.

Now's the time to explore what you really care about. Great accomplishments are the product of great passions. If you do not have a passion, find one. Reinvent yourself. Align yourself with something you care about, something that stirs the passions within, something that will embolden and enhance your senior years. Make a mind shift that focuses on the possibilities for a better life.

It's not as hard as you might think. Every mind shift starts with three easy steps:

1. Find ways to open new doors.
2. Make changes in your life that lay a foundation for future growth.
3. Research a variety of opportunities that excite your imagination.

Let me give you a dramatic example. Many years ago when I was a young vice president with Baskin-Robbins, I served on the advisory board of the Boston College Center for the Study of Franchise Distribution. Another member of that board was Ray Kroc, the founder of McDonald's. As many of you know, Ray began his amazing journey to the top of a franchise empire in his late fifties as a paper cup and mixer salesman. At an age when most people are looking for security, he took a monumental risk and cobbled together an investor group to buy the McDonald Brothers' franchising company for $2.7 million. The rest, of course, is history.

Ray once commented, "I was an overnight success all right, but thirty-plus years is a long, long night." At that time of his life when many people were winding down business careers, Ray was willing to take a risk—an enormous risk—to reinvent himself as a small business owner. Today McDonald's restaurants are everywhere, and the corporation's worldwide sales are astonishingly in excess of thirty billion dollars annually. Even Queen Elizabeth II owns a McDonald's franchise near Buckingham Palace.

But you don't have to sell thirty billion dollars' worth of cheeseburgers to realize a worthwhile ambition. Whether you decide to develop a for-profit corporation or a nonprofit organization, progress and achievement can follow if you become a change agent leader. That's someone who has vision, becomes a uniting force, and can sell an organization on the benefits of change and growth. Lots of people can keep a place going; only a change agent leader can take a company or organization to the Promised Land.

So, what's a change agent leader? First and foremost, this person is a *we* leader, someone who truly represents everyone in the organization. The opposite kind, an *I* leader, is so self-absorbed that over time he or she self-destructs and often destroys the organization as well.

If you are fortunate to work in an organization led by a *we* leader, enjoy the ride. When you retire, take all that you have learned and put it to work in your life and in your community. You will find that your leadership skills are appreciated, your contribution significant, and your personal rewards gratifying.

If, on the other hand, you are suffering in an organization with weak leadership, take action and move on! Reinvent yourself, bring excitement and joy back into your life, and find work that you love.

Black Night Journey

I tossed and turned last night,
my body roiling my restless mind.

Too many things undone
wrapped around missing pieces
and endless questions.

Yesterdays filled with mystic
travels to the far reaches of
consciousness searching the
philosopher's cabinet.

Journeys to Tibetan monasteries
and Jesuit retreats challenged by
existentialist passions.

Lying on a Roman terrace with
Cicero and Cato lamenting the
passing of their golden world.

Sailing with Byron and Shelley
on storm-filled Tyrrhenian Seas
searching for scraps of meaning
in a dissolute life.

Awakening in a peaceful Sardegna
Bay, with the gift of a sun-filled day
to seek new answers.

CHAPTER 3
THE COURAGE TO GROW

Life shrinks or expands in proportion
to one's courage.

–Anaïs Nin

A lot of people I know approach retirement with a sense of dread. They have served faithfully as corporate warriors, fought many successful battles with friends and enemies alike, and enjoyed the camaraderie of a well-led organization. The sense of community that work gives you, especially in corporate life, can be very seductive. Modern business has a lot of perks, but the most important is the sense of being part of something.

The prospect of losing this feeling, along with all the other benefits of working, can be profoundly depressing; yet few people plan for this loss. I have known many managers and executives who created nothing to replace their corporate lives when they retired, and they ended up feeling adrift. They left something behind and failed to create a new world to replace the one they lost. As a result they felt as if they had dropped into an abyss and were struggling to climb out.

Even those who had been looking forward to retirement can get that feeling. They celebrate the newfound freedom that had been missing from their career years but lament the loss of purpose and achievement that work provided. If you're feeling something similar, how can you replace what you're missing?

The answer, of course, is to create something that will be stimulating and personally rewarding when you retire. Entering the world of community service, starting a unique small business, accepting a teaching assignment at a community college, or developing a mentoring relationship with a young entrepreneur can give you that sense of purpose and achievement again.

Countless travel possibilities offer other adventures that can give you back that excitement you're missing. Opportunities to grow and expand your life are truly endless, but it takes courage to venture forth and seize them. It's not that important which path you choose; what matters is that you do *something* new and exciting.

Whatever you do, don't straddle the retirement fence thinking about what you might do and never getting around to it. While maintaining relationships and valuing old friends is certainly important, it is vital to get on with the new and exciting post-retirement life you desire.

I have seen many people in the professions maintain a post-retirement office in the partnership building. I'm sure this step helps a lot of people make the transition to retirement gracefully. Lawyers, for instance, need some time to wrap up cases and help long-standing clients develop relationships with new counsel. I've also seen how holding on to this last piece of professional life can make embracing a new post-retirement world much more difficult.

Sometimes your old colleagues can make it even more difficult. An attorney friend of mine soon grew tired of his quasi-departure arrangement and closed his retirement office because his partners and staff still went to such great lengths to keep him involved in the work of the partnership. He finally held a second retirement party to convince them he was really leaving.

Lifelong learning plays an important role in preparing you for a new life because you cannot embrace a new life without understanding what is required. For example, you might need to go back to school at a community college, art school, trade school, or even law school. At a minimum, you should research the Internet to develop a database supporting the direction you plan to travel and use a social network to talk to others familiar with the new life you hope to invent for yourself.

You can also start small with minor changes to your habits to open up new doors. You'd be amazed how much a new device can help. For instance, you could get a smartphone; or, if you've got one already, figure out how to use it. I know many people our age resisted the whole smartphone thing as yet another waste-of-time-fad, but it turns out that these tools can play a very special role in your life.

It helps to see a smartphone for what it really is: a phone that also connects you to the Internet. Recently this capability has become the gateway to the social networking websites and programs with unlimited possibilities for connecting with family, friends, and people who share your interests. If you connect your website or blog to a social network, it can increase your marketing and advertising reach enormously and for free.

When you travel, your smartphone can provide a portable office for checking on investments, trading stocks, conducting research, transferring money, and adjusting travel plans. Whether you're fond of new technology or not, the Internet has become the primary destination of the twenty-first century; and the chariot that will take you there rests in your pocket or purse. Learn how to use it wisely, and you will dramatically expand the possibilities of your senior years.

But all these possibilities rest on one key element: your financial plan. Most people have a consultant to assist in developing a sound platform to ensure financial security through the retirement years. Banks, accounting firms, and securities companies can also assist in retirement financial planning. When developing a plan, however, you need to face the unpleasant reality of life expectancy tables. These tables always carry good news and bad news. You've either got a lot of time, and you have to stretch the money farther; or you've got the opposite. (You can decide which one you prefer!) In any case life expectancy tables are an essential part of your financial plan and your reality check.

Moving on to more elevating thoughts, no one ever made an optimistic plan by spending an excessive amount of time contemplating mortality or money. Let's turn to our creative side. Most of us have a creative side that is underdeveloped. We may have explored it in school, but we abandoned it under the pressure of family life and earning a living.

In my own case, I was captivated by poetry and intrigued by its creative options and ability to communicate at a depth of understanding that I found exciting. After writing extensively as a young man, the pressures of my professional life—whether it was corporate management, teaching, consulting, or international business—slowed my career as a poet. Nevertheless I did read a lot of poetry and built a significant poetry library over the years, dreaming of what I might write if I had the time.

With my retirement from the corporate world, my creative inspiration resurfaced and became an important part of my life. Poetry may not be the art form you love the most, but your favorite art form can help the creative being inside you resurface. My wife Christine has rekindled her love of photography; and we even collaborated on a volume of poetry and photographs entitled *Love Shadows.*

Your new interests do not need to be so solitary or so stationary. One of the best ways to explore the culture and art of our diverse world is to travel. Last year my sister Kay and a friend from her years as a flight attendant went on a new journey together: a trip to Tuscany for an Italian cooking class. They expanded their culinary skills in Italian cuisine dramatically and enjoyed a marvelous cultural experience discovering the history, architecture, art, and music of this important center of the Renaissance.

Unfortunately many people have been so focused on their jobs, raising a family, putting their children through school, and taking care of others that they reach their senior years without knowing the excitement and joys of travel. Budget constraints also limit choices, and if you don't travel much you can become too timid to do it—there is an element of courage necessary for travel.

So work up your nerve and get going! You might want to start with some well-beaten but rewarding paths; and if you plan carefully, it doesn't have to cost too much money. If you have never been to Europe, go out of season when the airfares and hotel costs are dramatically lower. See Paris, Madrid, Rome, Athens, and the other destinations that will expand your cultural horizons. If you're feeling more adventurous, go to China or Latin America. If you're feeling a little less adventurous (or you need a cheaper alternative), explore America, especially if you've never done it. Visit all those places you have heard about and never experienced, from San Francisco to Boston. The beaches of California, the mountains of Colorado, the lakes of Minnesota, the rivers of Ohio, and the forests of Maine all welcome you. America waits to dazzle you and make you proud. Take tours, take cruises, and expand your horizons. Make your senior years a time of discovery.

If you're not inspired yet, let the great poet Alfred, Lord Tennyson help you. His poem "Ulysses" captures the essence of this opportunity. It's the voice of the aging king sitting safely on his throne in Ithaka, passing his days without purpose, as he gathers a few friends to embark on a journey of exploration one more time.

"Ulysses" by Alfred, Lord Tennyson
(excerpt)

…Come, my friends.
'Tis not too late to seek a newer world.
Push off, and sitting well in order smite
the sounding furrows; for my purpose holds
To sail beyond the sunset, and the baths
Of all the western stars, until I die.
It may be that the gulfs will wash us down;
It may be that we shall touch the Happy Isles,
And see the great Achilles, whom we knew.
Though much is taken, much abides; and though
We are not now that strength which in old days
Moved earth and heaven, that which we are, we are
One equal temper of heroic hearts,
Made weak by time and fate, but strong in will
To strive, to seek, to find, and not to yield.

I know that not everyone can explore the world as
a senior—health and finances can limit us—but for
those of us who have the will and the means, it can
open incredible doors to understanding our origins,
our cultural roots, and the evolving world scene. Sailing
beyond the sunset beckons. To help you discover your

next journey, whether artistic or geographic, I've added a place for you to write your *bucket list* at the end of the chapter, along with another of my poems.

> You will find poetry nowhere unless you
> bring some of it with you.
> –Joseph Joubert

MY BUCKET LIST PLUS

Expanding My Perspective

Places I would like to explore:

1. _____

2. _____

3. _____

4. _____

Things I would like to experience:

1. _____

2. _____

3. _____

4. _____

Author, Author

The occasion was a dear friend's
new book, published after an
arid hiatus of some twenty years.
A desert time when words lay
buried in the sand of some
far distant land.

Now, a rebirth with words
flowing once again. They would
arrive in the middle of the night,
in the heat of midday, or early
in an evening's sunset. A torrent
of words falling one upon another
in a cloudburst of thought.

The attention, while well-deserved
puzzled him, the plague of self
doubt still existed in the recesses
and corners of his mind. Was this
creative explosion the end? Was
this naught but a writer's death knell?

I comforted him as best I could,
reassuring him that this rebirth was
truly a beginning. The phoenix had
arisen from the ashes to fly to
distant shores, to carry him to places
of which he could only dream.

CHAPTER 4
THE GOOD NEWS: VOLUNTEER OPPORTUNITIES ARE EVERYWHERE

> Happiness is when what you think, what you say,
> and what you do are in harmony.
> –Mahatma Gandhi

If you worked hard at your career, you probably didn't have much time for volunteering. Now that you've retired, you can get involved in your community in a new and satisfying way. Educational, cultural, and social service organizations play a key role in determining the quality of life and the health of communities across America, but those organizations could not survive and prosper without the services of hundreds of thousands of volunteers. Docents in museums, volunteer gardeners in botanical gardens, financial experts serving on nonprofit investment committees, and board members and trustees for charitable organizations: these and many more types of volunteers perform vital services to our communities.

Now that you've got the time, you have an abundance of opportunities to make a difference. Community nonprofits need lots of different kinds of people with different skill sets, but all of them can use the judgment, experience, and managerial skill that you can provide. You can almost certainly find an opportunity to serve that will give you a sense of doing something important and highly valued.

Despite the differences between the for-profit and nonprofit worlds, seniors with acquired skills in the business world often find a number of opportunities to put their skills to work. You may be reluctant to make a commitment to a nonprofit organization after so many years of being tied to your job, but it's worth taking the plunge once you've considered the pros and cons of a particular volunteering opportunity.

I have to admit that nonprofits have some challenges that you generally don't find in the business world. One retired executive shared confidentially with me that he did not have the patience to sit through long nonprofit board meetings. With no time-is-money profit motive, the board members would talk endlessly about matters of little importance.

Other volunteer board members have told me that these meetings often spend too much time on trivial issues, too. I'm afraid that this problem is just part of the landscape in the volunteer world, and I strongly recommend that nonprofits consider this criticism when developing their agendas. But that's also an issue with nonprofit organizations that sharp, experienced managers like you can help fix. Nothing revitalizes a sleepy organization like having a few no-nonsense, motivated people come onboard.

You also should not let the fact that you have not been involved with an organization before deter you from joining it. You would be amazed at the range of organizations that would welcome you.

In every community there are hundreds of nonprofit organizations providing a variety of services to their citizens. For example, in my community of Santa Barbara County, there are over seventeen hundred nonprofits providing a variety of services. These organizations include those supporting the disadvantaged and others involved with education, medical, cultural arts, animal welfare, and environmental issues.

Some of the national organizations you may find in your community include the United Way, American Red Cross, Direct Relief, Humane Society, Dream Foundation, YMCA, Boys and Girls Club, Big Brother, Big Sister, Sierra Club, zoological societies, Alzheimer's Association, Habitat for Humanity, Special Olympics, American Cancer Society, Visiting Nurse Association, Hospice, Food Bank, Braille Institute, SEE International, and the March of Dimes.

Serving your community doesn't just mean working with nonprofit organizations. Many people enter local politics after retiring. If you think that you can do a better job that your current local politicians, you can run for city council, mayor, the school board, the state assembly, district supervisor, or even the US House of Representatives.

The United States has a long and honorable tradition of people who have acquired skills in business life participating in politics. Political life can give you a chance to take your acquired wisdom and organizational skills and offer them to your community in a direct and visible way. Every political organization has a need for a wise man or woman. Step up and make a difference.

Your community has a wealth of opportunities to serve, if you know how to see them. I hear many people decry the lack of opportunities where they live, but they're wrong. They just have poor vision. They fail to recognize that opportunities missed are often ones not recognized when they pass by for review. My brother Jim once said to me regarding his friend who seemed to be on a treadmill to nowhere, "He wouldn't recognize an opportunity if it came up and hit him upside the head with a two by four." That's sage wisdom from the Midwest, and it's useful anywhere.

Not only do you have to recognize the opportunities, but you must pursue them aggressively. If you want to be on the board or committee of a nonprofit, you have to let that organization know of your interest. You should not stand on the sidelines waiting to be discovered. Even becoming a fan or supporter of an organization that you really like could lead to something more.

Nonprofit organizations typically have a diverse number of committees that perform key functions for the organization. In an organization like Lotus-land, a botanical garden in Santa Barbara, you can work as a docent, volunteer gardener, investment advisor, fundraiser, board member, or member of the special events or personnel committee, and on and on. Surely you can find something to do that makes a valuable contribution to the nonprofit and to the community.

Side by Side

They had been together
                for too many years
        survivors
Their journey traversed the earth
                exploring new lands
        then circling back
Intent on seeking out
                what might have been
        missed
Following primitive rivers
                into the depths
        of the Amazon green
Running across the sands
                of abandoned beaches
        discovering lost islands
Always, adventurers pushing aside old
                failures, finding new dreams
        side by side

CHAPTER 5
MANAGING THE PHYSICAL DEMANDS OF AN ACTIVE SENIOR LIFE

Some people, no matter how old they get,
never lose their beauty—they merely
move it from their faces into their hearts.

–Martin Buxbaum

For decades, Americans have been obsessed with maintaining a youthful appearance beyond anything the previous generation could have imagined. Antiaging creams and emollients dominate the cosmetic departments of stores and Internet offerings. In 2010 alone, eight hundred and thirty-two million consumers used antiaging creams; and thirteen million obtained cosmetic procedures. Somehow people have convinced themselves that a youthful appearance will actually slow the aging process. Toni Calasanti, PhD, a sociology professor at Virginia

Tech, stated in a recent issue of *AARP The Magazine,* "Since looking old affects our social status, we want to keep passing for younger." As a result, "We dye our hair, watch our weight, bleach our teeth, and cover up facial lines with cosmetics or smooth them out with plastic surgery. Medical intervention has gone from questionable to acceptable: half of all Americans, regardless of income, now say they approve of it."

I know a number of women in my community who have had second or third facelifts. Go ahead and look your best, but remember that time marches on no matter what.

Acknowledging this simple truth will give you some peace of mind in an era gone slightly mad. According to Debra Sellers, PhD, a professor at Kansas State University, "Our preoccupation with looking younger… suggests there's something wrong with the aging process. Focusing only on loss implies that individuals who are aging are less of who they once were, and it fosters negative societal stereotypes of older adults." In other words, the natural process of aging has now become a kind of disease, as if living a long time were something that you need to cure.

Of course I like to look as youthful as I can, too—don't get me wrong. I believe that a more youthful appearance can lift your spirits, especially if you're experiencing a midlife crisis. But as you go beyond midlife into your senior years, you have to come to terms with reality. As the saying goes, "Beauty is only skin deep." Instead of worrying excessively about a youthful appearance, give some thought instead to maintaining a youthful outlook. That's what truly aging gracefully is about. Embrace new ideas, explore new ways of life, and embark on new careers. Fill each day with all that life has to offer. Even now I chastise myself for all that I am passing up, yet I am experiencing more than most.

You may well ask how all this youthful activity is possible. In literal terms, what makes all this possible are dramatic advances in the field of medical science. We can do more now because we live longer and hold on to more of our physical and mental capabilities later in life.

But these advances cause some problems, too. When President Franklin D. Roosevelt established the Social Security Administration, life expectancy was almost the same as retirement age; and fewer retirees managed to collect their benefits. Nobody anticipated that life expectancies would increase by almost a decade and a half, as they have done recently. This problem is a great challenge to the nation, and we should all take it seriously.

But for now, we will just address the challenges that you and I face as seniors. We are living longer, but are we taking advantage of the added years and living well? To do that you must maintain a healthier lifestyle than your parents and grandparents did. The added years of senior and super senior life that medical science have given you will not be years of living well unless you do your part.

But don't worry. It's not that hard. You don't have to go into bodybuilding; just do some regular, moderate exercise. For instance, when my wife and I travel, we often rent bikes to explore the area we are visiting. I have good friends who walk every morning; another couple swims every day. We have found that the key is to exercise regularly. Even a half hour spent four times a week on a stationary bike can go a long way toward keeping a senior healthy.

Of course you have to do what your doctor tells you. Take your prescribed medications as directed and have a comprehensive annual physical examination. Regular checkups can help you detect an illness early and make treatment much easier and more effective. Good nutrition is more important now than ever. Vitamin deficiencies can play havoc with your immune system, and you need it to be working optimally.

Don't give in to the temptation to slack off now that you're older. A health regimen is the key to maintaining your physical well-being and enjoying the experience of your senior years to the greatest degree possible. You must accept responsibility for managing yourself and your partner so that you can face the physical challenges of advanced years.

Good overall health can also help you maintain a constructive, healthful, sensual life with your partner. Don't hesitate to tell your partner how much you care. Your energy and attention to your partner will make a vital contribution to emotional stability and provide positive support for your relationship. Some seniors have difficulty demonstrating their affection for a partner of many years, but this doesn't have to be the case for you. Take advantage of opportunities to get away for a romantic weekend to support your intimacy. A sensual, caring, supportive relationship can fill senior years with much joy.

But we also have to recognize that as we live longer, one of the partners will be incapacitated by illness. When this terrible day comes, the burden on the caregiver partner can be overwhelming. If you have the financial means to plan for such an eventuality, you should do it. If other members of the family can assume some of the caregiver burden, both partners will have a more positive experience.

Regardless of where you stand on the question of an afterlife, preparing for death, taking care of the care of the sick and dying, and mourning lost loved ones will always remain at the center of the pain and mystery of existence. With that in mind, it might be helpful for us, as members of the six thousand sunrises club, to reimagine the roles we could play in these crucial matters. As people live longer and more robustly than ever before, we should be able to apply the active wisdom of Adulthood Two to the reality of death in new and more spiritual ways.

Ultimately, spirituality is about what people do for one another. Now that we have the time and wisdom to participate more fully in the community than before, we stand a better chance of both giving and receiving the kind of compassion that we all need as we face mortality. Can we take away the hypocrisy and denial our society weaves around the end of life and replace it with something smarter and more honest?

We will all face our death eventually, but only some of us will face the pain of losing a beloved partner. If you are the survivor, take the time to mourn, then return to an active, involved life and once again experience the benefits of working to assist those in your community who are less fortunate. The gratitude for assistance offered can make you feel that your role in society is important and highly valued.

It may seem odd, but I'd like to finish this somewhat somber chapter by saying that humor can make an important contribution to your sense of well-being. If you can enjoy a good laugh at some of the vagaries of life, you can add years to your life span. Regardless of the challenges we face, most of us can find something to laugh about even in the darkest of times.

You don't stop laughing because you grow old.
You grow old because you stop laughing.
                              –Maurice Chevalier

Take Me to the Country

Let me see the greens
the yellows and reds
the browns and golds
let them course swiftly
through my veins in a
sensual transfusion

Let me smell apple orchards
and wheat fields, cow barns
and cloud reaching silos
of fresh picked corn

Let me hear the cricket
the hummingbird, the honey bee
the singing of the combine
the laughter at the table

Let me feel the freshness
of times long past
when my grandfather worked
with his sons in the bean field
and God blessed
our daily lives

Let me taste the harvests
and revel in their sweetness

Let me touch your body
and know its natural kindness

We'll have our children there

CHAPTER 6
PROCESSING YOUR SPIRITUAL NEEDS

Just as a candle cannot burn without fire,
men cannot live without a spiritual life.

–Buddha

As we age we start feeling the need to come back to God. You have probably had the feeling that showing up at church or a synagogue at the end of the week might help ensure an afterlife, even if you haven't been there for a while. But I'm sure you know that attendance is just that, merely showing up.

True spirituality asks more of us.

Spirituality requires that we live our lives with an appreciation for our role in the betterment of humankind. We must recognize that we are all connected. When we have an opportunity to help someone in a time of need, we are responding to our connectivity with those who have passed before us as well as those who follow. Whether we follow Jesus Christ, Jehovah, Buddha, or Mohammed, their teachings focus on our responsibility for others. When religions become the basis for contempt and prejudice, they lose touch with humanity.

As I am sure you've noticed, the demographic represented by the six thousand sunrises generation coincides with a profound, interesting, and complex change in Americans' attitudes toward religion and spirituality. Even as people seem to be fleeing traditional forms of religious observance because of scandal and disillusionment, a greater awareness of spirituality has been overtaking the country. But the fact that fewer people attend church services does not mean that there is a dearth of spirituality. In fact, this departure from business as usual in religious matters has awakened a personal sense of what is spiritual in many people.

Despite popular conceptions about the selfishness of the baby boomers, many members of this generation derive significant sustenance from helping others. That's where they go for their spirituality not to churches, synagogues, and mosques but to soup kitchens, shelters, AIDS Walks, or holiday toy drives.

As opportunities to express charity expand beyond the boundaries of traditional religious organizations and multiply across social divisions, more and more people experience the essence of spirituality as giving back to the community.

You should also keep in mind that you have a special responsibility toward the community with regard to its spiritual welfare. Whether you have anticipated this role or not, your status as a member of an older generation gives you the task of handing down a spiritual legacy to those who come after you. As you pass through your senior years, others will look to you for wisdom as an elder in our society. In virtually all cultures, elders are revered, sought out for their counsel, and respected for their spirituality and the knowledge they have gained. Since 1966 Japan has actually celebrated an annual Respect for the Aged Day.

A few months ago, an acquaintance of mine told me a wonderful story. Two men who had worked with him many years before came to see him, despite infrequent contact with him over the years. They were starting a new company and faced a number of ethical issues. They came to him because they respected him and needed his guidance. They knew they could trust him for his ethical and spiritual leadership and remembered how in difficult times they could always count on him to do the right thing.

Spiritual responsibilities have migrated from traditional religious settings to other places in many instances; and as these changes occur, civic organizations will look to older members of the community for guidance.

At a recent planning meeting of a community foundation, a group of trustees searched for a theme for their long-range plan. It was first suggested that a moral compass might play a role in their thinking, but they still needed something more specific. Then a senior suggested that "love of your fellow humans" might provide such a focus. This simple line, in my view, represented a shift from the secular to the spiritual that redirected the thinking of the group toward traditional religious values and gave its members a renewed sense of purpose. If the love of your fellow humans becomes a moral compass, then kindness will surely follow.

Recently a good friend of mine referred to me as an extraordinarily kind man. I was embarrassed because, while I value kindness highly, I found myself thinking of the many unkind things I have done. Perhaps, as I have grown older, I have in fact become kinder. I hope so since the relationship of loving one's fellow humans and becoming more kind can play a significant part in becoming more spiritual as you travel through your senior years.

I know it may be hard to think in such positive terms when the news reports so many bad things. Almost every day we seem to read about unimaginably unethical behavior. Politicians regularly flunk the character test as they seek office, while corporate executives walk a narrow line between right and wrong, and often fall onto the wrong side. They think, "If it is even borderline legal, then it must be okay to proceed." But the concept of right or wrong requires more than a legal scale of measurement; it requires a true ethical review that only long experience can provide.

As elders in our society, we have a moral obligation to pass judgment on corporate and governmental behavior when it flies in the face of the moral and ethical standards of right and wrong that we know from many situations over many years. Speak out, attend community meetings, write letters to the editor, and communicate with your representatives in Washington. Make yourself heard!

Tuscan Morning

The sun awakened
to a lavender day
and raised a wary eye
then blinked
a yellow sky.
The Tuscan roof tiles
far below
sent their orange reflection
blazing across
the cold morning.
The hillside vineyards
reached out for the
day's warm caress
as the bells of San Gregorio
pealed out in
joyous rapture.
Once again God
had given his blessing
to his chosen ones.

CHAPTER 7
CHALLENGES TO THE NEW YOU

Every man takes the limits of his own field of vision
for the limits of the world.
–Arthur Schopenhauer

Life is about discovery, surprise, and blazing
your own trail.
–Mahatma Gandhi

I'm sure you already know how long-range strategic planning helps businesses. Every enterprise can benefit from of a vision of the future. This plan provides a catalyst for operational planning and helps everything run successfully. But have you considered what your vision of yourself ten years into the future will look like? If you have painted such a picture of your own future, what do you need to do today to make that vision a reality?

Strategic planning involves asking a lot of questions, both big and small. First, what *is* your vision of the future? What would you like your retirement years to look like? What experiences would you like to have? What would you like to accomplish? How would you like to live? What would you like to look like? What *suit* would you like to wear?

Even broad answers to those questions can lead you to the actions you should take right now. What can you do today to start this journey that will fill your senior and super senior years with personal fulfillment and continuing accomplishments? Your rewarding new life won't happen by accident. You have to imagine it, plan it, and appreciate it to make it real.

As I've said before, reinventing yourself will require you to take some risks. You will need courage. You will have to leave your comfort zone. In one way or another, you will have to explore the unknown. But all of these dramatic actions begin with one small step: taking charge of your destiny. Many people aren't up to the task. But if you are, you'll find that the rewards will far outweigh the risks; and you'll be on your way to achieving a remarkable senior and super senior life.

The transformation of your life as a senior has an important precedent in the Bible. In Genesis, when God told Abraham that his wife Sarah would bear a child despite her old age, they laughed because such an event was beyond what they could imagine. But God had told the truth, and their son Isaac eventually became a patriarch of the tribes of Israel.

Now your own miracle probably won't be the same, but this story strikes a chord with many of us. If you find yourself thinking, "I'm too old for any new possibilities," remember this story and think again. The world is full of everyday miracles. The possibilities you face in these golden, sunlit senior years are endless. You just need to open your mind to what might yet be and pursue your possibilities with passion.

Passion plays a key role in planning. If you are passionate about the path you are pursuing, you will follow it with enthusiasm, confidence, and unbridled joy. I have seen people go through the motions of living as they wound down their preretirement years only to be totally transformed as they reinvented themselves and became engaged in pursuing newly discovered or previously suppressed passionate endeavors in retirement.

Many times I heard them say something like this: "I have put in my time doing what someone else wanted me to do. Now that I am retired and free, I have the opportunity to engage in something I really care about!" If you can say the same thing, you will enjoy the fruits of a passion pursued and realized as a significant accomplishment. So don't pass up the opportunity. Focus all your energy on making a difference in your senior years by chasing dreams previously laid aside.

Does that sound too exhausting for you at this age? It isn't if you can stay young in spirit. The easiest way to do that is to find ways to associate with younger people and expose yourself to their thinking and attitudes. Senior citizen residences are often wonderful places, but unfortunately they surround you with people of the same generation. Finding ways of building relationships with younger people through involvement with schools and youth organizations such as the Boys and Girls Clubs, church youth groups, athletic teams, etc. will freshen your spirit in your new, expanded life.

Sometimes you don't have to go far to find young people. You can have one more child of your own, even without divine intervention. I found that having a teenage son during my seventies was an incredibly rewarding experience.

Like many people, I loved and enjoyed my first family; but the children were grown when I married my second wife, Christine. At first she and I had no plans for children, but as time passed Christine found herself longing for the experience. So I agreed. Little did I realize the role this child would play in keeping me young in spirit and with renewed vitality! I was constantly being exposed to the excitement and challenges of youth: attending soccer and volleyball games, traveling to new places, experiencing new relationships and literature, listening to new music, and even suffering through SAT preparation and college selection.

Of course this life pattern doesn't happen to everyone, and for a lot of people one set of children per lifetime is sufficient. Still you can develop a rewarding relationship by mentoring a grandchild or a friend's child who needs help. Recently I guided my grandson through his college selection process. It was a wonderful experience for me that brought us much closer as a result.

The task of finding the new you for your senior sunrise years can prove to be challenging; but if you use all the tools available, you will be surprised at your success. Just remember that you are the product of all the choices you have made in life, both good and bad. As you look forward to your six thousand sunrises, once again you will be making choices. Give these opportunities for creating the new you the attention they deserve. Don't just let things happen. Make the choices that will support and deliver the new you that you desire.

Finally, be prepared to make other important choices as you pursue your vision. We live in a dynamic world of change, and we must be prepared to regularly examine our vision in light of the evolving circumstances.

VISION PLANNING

Looking ten years into the future:

1. What work would I like to be doing?

_____

_____

_____

_____

_____

2. Where would I like to be living?

_____

_____

_____

_____

_____

3. What travel would I like to be experiencing?

_____

_____

_____

_____

_____

4. What creative interests would I like to be pursuing and enjoying?

    _____

    _____

    _____

    _____

    _____

5. What organizations that benefit other people would I like to be playing a valued role in supporting?

    _____

    _____

    _____

    _____

    _____

6. What family experiences would I like to be enjoying?

    _____

    _____

    _____

    _____

    _____

7. How will I be mentoring and assisting young family members and friends to find constructive ways to live and contribute to society?

_____

_____

_____

_____

_____

8. How will I have educated myself to be better prepared to live a complete life in my future time zone?

_____

_____

_____

_____

_____

Celebration

Let's celebrate life
and find our freedom
with the exultation
of knowing ourselves
through each other.

Help me touch the sun
and I'll share with you
fresh meadows at Yosemite,
tall redwoods and wild blackberries,
cold mountain streams in Oregon.

Help me swallow the ocean
and I'll share with you
quiet anchorages at Santa Cruz,
raindrops on port windows,
billowing warm spinnaker rainbows.

Help me catch the eagle
and I'll share with you
lazy summer afternoons in Kent,
antiques and polished silver,
tea and soft string quartets.

Come celebrate life
and cover yourself
with today's joy,
unlike brothers Sartre and Camus,
we'll plan for great tomorrows.

CHAPTER 8
FAMILY ISSUES: INTRODUCING YOUR FAMILY TO CONSTRUCTIVE CHANGE

Call it a clan, call it a network, call it a tribe,
call it a family. Whatever you call it,
whoever you are, you need one.

–Jane Howard

I know why families were created with all their
imperfections. They humanize you. They are
made to make you forget yourself occasionally so
that the beautiful balance of life is not destroyed.

–Anaïs Nin

Y ou are not the only one who finds adjusting to your new life as a senior challenging. Your family does, too. They have become accustomed to dealing with you in stable, predictable ways; and now that you are making some significant life changes, they can feel threatened. Relationships and roles established over many years can change suddenly and in surprising ways. One of your children might wonder, "Who is this person who used to be my father?" When they see a parent exploring new dreams, traveling new roads, and making new friends, children can often become defensive and overprotective.

To understand what's really going on, try looking at the situation from the family's point of view. Some years ago, I was having lunch with a friend who was obviously agitated. When I asked him what was wrong, he said he was having parental problems. His eighty-four-year-old parents had purchased a piece of land and were building a new home some hundred and fifty miles away in a seaside town. He had discovered the whole plan by accident; they had not discussed the project with him at all. I asked if they were moving soon, and he said he did not know.

I said how wonderful it was that they would have the joy of creating a new home their family could enjoy for many years after they were gone. He looked surprised and said, "I never thought of it that way." My friend had been looking at his parents from the perspective of an overly protective child, who thought that by keeping them in a box with predictable behavior he could keep them safe.

He said he was worried about their health and whether someone might take advantage of them. I responded that he should visit them and tell them how wonderful it was that they were creating this new special place and to let them know he was there if they needed him. He followed my advice and sent me a bottle of champagne after his visit, which turned out to be a joyous experience for all concerned.

Seniors need to have their independence respected; they need to be encouraged to enjoy the fruits of their senior years. Their families have to understand the changes they are experiencing and create a balance between support and freedom. Keep the lines of communication open as you make your changes, and you'll find that your family will probably be encouraging and enthusiastic.

But you can face problems, too. Seniors, particularly super seniors, can sometimes encounter a surprising lack of respect from younger family members, even about relatively trivial matters. For instance, younger family members who have grown up in the technology age often will not appreciate the challenges that seniors face dealing with the latest gadget. Explain patiently that, while we may not adapt as quickly as we used to, we will adapt.

Keep in mind that respect is a two-way street. While we seniors want our desire for independence to be respected, we need to respect the fact that generational differences can lead to different perspectives. This is particularly apparent if you consider that the curriculum when we were in school may have been utterly different from the curriculum for the generations that followed. Seniors often require and deserve a substantial serving of patience and understanding, but our younger counterparts are only human, too. "Cut your elders some slack" might be a worthwhile mantra for young adults interacting with senior family members, and "cut your juniors some slack" might be a worthwhile mantra for seniors.

You can also run into some difficulties with your partner now that the natural independence of the separation between your work and home life has come to an end. After you retire you may find that you are suddenly perceived as underfoot in your own house. "I married you for better or worse but not for lunch" has a ring of truth in a changing relationship.

So keep your eyes and ears open for this adjustment and enjoy the positive aspects of suddenly having more potential time together with a spouse who might have felt somewhat neglected before your retirement. In the end, life partners need to find a good balance between respecting each other's independence and enjoying each other's company as they make plans for moving forward.

The world has made this balancing act even harder in recent years. When both partners work, they tend to exist as a couple through a series of fragmented mutual experiences. I've even heard a busy couple say, "Isn't that great? We will both be in Chicago at the same time next week."

When both partners retire somewhat simultaneously, they can feel as if they are starting over. But they're not—at least not as a couple—and that's the key to getting on with your new life. If you and your partner can respect each other's past—how you worked and lived over the many years it took to get to this point—you'll both have a better chance of understanding how to make the compromises essential for the future.

Those compromises are worth making, believe me. Entering your retirement years requires an appreciation for the poetry of a sensitive, caring family life. You should find it and cherish it. But you should also keep in mind that relationships—and families—are always changing, and that's a good thing. The dynamics of the evolving family can be transformational.

Relationships between parents and children and between siblings evolve as each family member has new experiences. Additionally, exposure to each other ebbs and flows over time; and there are no guarantees that a family separated by thousands of miles will maintain close, caring relationships.

There is also a major role reversal that not everyone anticipates. As parents age and require greater assistance, the children can suddenly become the caregivers. When everything changes in this way, adjusting requires work on everybody's part.

It is especially important for families to *decide* to keep their relationships going. For many years my parents had kept their five children connected, despite our being scattered all over the country. When our parents died, my siblings and I made a pact that we would all spend a week together with our families every two years. For twenty-eight years, we have maintained that tradition, including a marvelous Thanksgiving week when forty-eight of us from ages nine months to ninety years spent a joy-filled week together in St. Augustine, Florida.

But these experiences do not happen without planning and family leadership. In our family we have rotated that leadership role among the original siblings, and we go to great lengths to share expenses so that no one is excessively burdened.

Despite our best efforts, time takes its toll on families, particularly the more commonly small-sized families of today. Death and other factors, such as military service or family conflict, can create a void in your life at the very time that you need family love the most. You should always be willing to reexamine and restore family relationships that have become withered and brittle with the passing of years. You may find it hard to breathe new life into a long dormant relationship, but it is well worth the effort.

Sometimes even the best efforts to reunite a family fail, especially when there are deep-rooted problems. If your family remains dysfunctional despite many attempts to make it work, you have the option of creating your own new family. If you can reinvent yourself, you can reinvent your family!

Expand your circle of close friends. You can shower them with familial affection and spend more time with these people you enjoy and care about. You can welcome friends who share their love, kindness, and caring for one another into your family—it's your family after all! These people will support you over the passage of years. If you recognize the importance of these special friends and allow them to play a larger, more important role in your family life, it can all work out wonderfully.

In the twenty-first century, this kind of reinvented family could well become the new norm as traditional family relationships with stifling expectations are challenged and, in some cases, abandoned. Whatever you do, take an active role in creating the family life you truly want and deserve.

the dawning

you bring the dawn
to my winter's night

carrying the atrophied
dreams of tomorrow

from their long
abandoned place

back to the edge
of today's reality

taking my tired temerity
by the hand

and leading it from
its place of hiding

into the early morning
light of what

might still yet be

CHAPTER 9
HOW YOU CAN MAKE A DIFFERENCE
IN THE LIVES OF OTHERS

The really important thing is not to live,
but to live well.

–Socrates

A life well lived can earn you some of the privileges of success. You may think I'm talking about golf club memberships, yachts, or trips around the world and I am but I am also thinking of what I consider to be perhaps the greatest privilege, which is the opportunity to help others.

Nothing contributes to your sense of self-worth in the senior years, or any other time of life for that matter, like making a difference in the lives of others. What's more, you don't have to give up everything else to do it. We're not all Mother Teresa nor are we meant to be. Small changes in your approach to life can mean big benefits to others if you think creatively and stay active. My friends, family, and I have had some wonderful chances to make a difference. You can do similar things, and you will feel better about yourself for having done them.

Earlier in my senior life, for instance, I had a wonderful experience helping others climb out of the poverty cycle when I chaired the Food Industry Crusade Against Hunger, a grant-making organization that supported efforts to alleviate hunger over the longer term. The organization didn't distribute food itself but instead funded efforts to help people overcome poverty through job creation and support. This organization helped a number of people improve their lives in real, substantial ways.

Let me show you two projects that demonstrate this program's impact. The organization funded a micro bank in Latin America that made small loans to women who were starting or operating their own businesses. In one case a mother who did piecework in her home took out a loan to buy a second sewing machine for her teenage daughter. This small project doubled their family income and allowed the mother to send her younger son to school. They paid back a loan for $250 in eighteen months. That was a real anti-poverty program!

Closer to home the Food Industry Crusade Against Hunger funded a job-creation program in the San Francisco Bay Area. The program selected men in a homeless shelter for a culinary skills training program. After training, these formerly down-and-out men were selected for positions at Bay Area restaurants. Volunteers drove them to work and subsequently monitored their job performances until they became independent, functioning citizens. The failure rate was less than ten percent over a two-year period.

Lots of other organizations around the country perform well-designed, useful services that help people improve their lives. Many communities have organizations like Santa Barbara's Transition House, which focuses on providing shelter and support for families that are homeless and trying to get back on their feet. Across the country, Habitat for Humanity creates shelter and long-term support for the needy. The Community Action Commission provides similar services, helping more than twelve thousand people each year achieve and maintain self-sufficiency.

It is very gratifying to find ways to assist people who are struggling with poverty and desperate to become self-sustaining. While providing sustenance to the hungry is vital, funding those programs seeking long-term answers is just as important. Reaching out to help others escape poverty is truly a spiritual act. As a senior or super senior, you undoubtedly have numerous opportunities to volunteer and make significant contributions to the lives of the underprivileged in your community.

Addressing the problem of poverty may not be your first or best choice for the kind of assistance you would like to lend in your senior years, but that doesn't mean you have to miss out on the benefits of helping others. An attorney of my acquaintance was diagnosed with Parkinson's disease when he was entering his seventies, and it hit him hard. He was just beginning his retirement, and suddenly many of the satisfactions he had anticipated those rounds of golf, sailing his boat, even just walking the beach near his home were more difficult and less pleasurable than he hoped.

At first the adjustment was a painful one, as he had been a very active person throughout his life; and the prospect of days devoid of either work or pleasure weighed heavily on him. Yet all was not lost. Although he had agreed with his former partners that, because of his condition, it would be inadvisable for him to practice law, another opportunity presented itself. Through a former colleague, he discovered that he could volunteer his time to serve as an impartial mediator for people who could not afford to take their legal issues to court.

The role of mediator in negotiations was one he had relished throughout his career; and now, in the early stages of Parkinson's, he found that he could still be of service in this capacity. It was truly a lifesaver for this man, and he continued to serve as a mediator until he could no longer do so. Even as a terrible disability encroached on his life, he found satisfaction in this important field because the work he did mattered and the people he helped were grateful.

As you can see from these stories, the opportunity to make a difference in the lives of others should be considered a great privilege and treated as such. As I chart the rivers of my retirement years, I realize how important it is to seek out opportunities to help others. It is extraordinarily rewarding. It will improve your self-image and contribute to your mental health and sense of well-being.

MAKING A DIFFERENCE

Where I have made a difference in the past.

1._____

2._____

3._____

4._____

5._____

Where I will strive to make a difference in the future.

1._____

2._____

3._____

4._____

5._____

conspirators

the morning crackled
electricity in the air
the sun charged
over the horizon
and threw its arms
around the day
breathing new life
into the darkness
it was a time when
each day had to be
lived as though
it was their last
every moment savored
the sun and the sea
conspiring to give them
a new beginning
they held its promise
in their desire

CHAPTER 10
EMBRACE THE REAL AFTERLIFE

To know how to grow old is the master-work of
wisdom, and one of the most difficult chapters
in the great art of living.

–Henri Frederic Amiel

As consoling and uplifting as the idea of a life after death has been for millions of people over the course of many centuries, you should think of the real afterlife that starts here and now while you are still alive and kicking. Life after retirement doesn't have to be a letdown. Make it a step up instead. When you look at the prospect of the many thousands of sunrises that you will experience during your senior years, you should feel excited by the opportunity to shape your life so that you enjoy the maximum possible degree of self-fulfillment.

I've discussed previously how work can bring you great satisfaction and joy, and our society recognizes the importance of work as a basis for personal achievement and satisfaction. In fact this combination of personal and social reward drives our economy almost as much as anything else. But if you enjoy your work and others appreciate your efforts, then why retire? Why not continue to work in this positive, nurturing environment? With life expectancy expanding significantly over recent decades and if you are in good health, why not remain in a positive work environment and postpone retirement?

This idea is certainly worth considering, especially these days. The financial benefits are clear: you can enhance your retirement income substantially by extending your active work life, with benefits accruing both in your private retirement plan and in Social Security. Many people are pursuing this option. A recent Employee Benefit Research Institute retirement conference survey reports a record 74 percent of not-yet-retired people expect to continue working for pay in retirement.

You can use this extended work life to plan for the afterlife when you eventually do retire. You can also involve yourself now in the nonprofits that serve your interests and begin to build the base for a successful retirement.

But when you do finally retire, you still need to find work substitutes that will provide similar personal rewards, including part-time work and unpaid positions. Remember these substitutes are about the personal, not the financial, rewards.

For instance, a retired accountant may find an opportunity to mentor a start-up entrepreneur who lacks financial skills and can benefit from the retired accountant's experience and judgment. A retired nurse might volunteer or accept a part-time position with an group like the Visiting Nurse and Hospice Care organization. A former professional athlete might become the coach of a high school team, a position where his or her experience would be highly valued. A retired teacher might volunteer for an afternoon tutoring program for the Boys and Girls Club.

These positions can give you some marvelous ways to get involved with your community on a new level. Involvement in areas that benefit people directly can be highly rewarding and expand an interest that you already have. If you love gardening, why not share that interest? Volunteer to maintain a garden at a community center or the local botanical garden and you'll find that others appreciate your time, energy, and skills.

Honestly, the alternative to finding fulfillment in retirement is bleak. Many retirees experience a great sense of loss when they finish their careers because they haven't found anything to fill the void. The wife of a recently retired corporate executive said to me, "Don feels like he drove off a cliff and is in free fall since he retired." When I saw him a few months later and asked how things were going, Don said, "I hate retirement." Why did he feel this way? The reason is clear: when Don retired, he left something behind and failed to create an afterlife.

In fact he should have begun the process at least five years before his actual retirement. Instead he experienced a shrinking of his life and self-worth because he had lost his basis for measuring achievement. Don is a smart, talented guy and had many avenues to pursue; but he needed to attack his post-retirement years with the same energy and commitment he gave to his corporate work. So don't you make the same mistake. "Be all that you can be" is as great a slogan for the retiree as it is for the United States Army!

As you travel through your senior years, you should stop at different times to reflect on the memories of people, places, and special moments that you have accumulated during your lifetime. Rushing from day to day without giving yourself time to gain perspective robs you of enjoying all you have experienced. In fact moving from one day to another without reflecting on how each day fits into your personal history represents a shallow existence. I don't want to sound too harsh, but I think you should ask yourself a very important question. How do you plan to reflect on your past journeys so that those memories can add color and dimension to the present?

The big point is that looking forward to your senior years also means looking back from time to time and integrating the past with the present in significant ways. My wife and I began a recent day by remembering a magical trip we once took to Europe.

We talked about every foolish thing we did and every wonderful place we visited, and just talking about it was almost as much fun as doing it the first time. Punctuated with much humor and good feelings, we thought about the impact that trip had on the direction of our lives. We knew that the distance of time and experience had changed our perspective on many things, but remembering the impact that long-ago trip had on both our lives added a special dimension to how we approach and experience each passing day.

Now that you have retired, you might think about relocating and finding a place more conducive to living your new life to the fullest. Certain smaller communities promote peace, harmony, and thoughtfulness more than others. They are often near the sea, in the mountains, or in farm country: towns like St. Michael's Island near Washington, DC; Portsmouth, New Hampshire, near Boston; or St. Helena near San Francisco. These places are wonderful getaways from the hustle and clamor of a large city.

You may also desire to maintain your home location but spend more time on weekend or summer retreats in these nourishing environments. My wife and I do this kind of thing often, and we enjoy visiting these places again and again. We like the people there with whom we develop casual relationships; often they remember our names and ask about our children. These communities help us find peace and reflect on the lives we lead. We find the familiarity of these places reassuring and restorative.

Now it's time for you to find your own peace. List the places (ports) you presently visit that bring you special enjoyment, places that you would like to experience on a regular basis.

1. _____

2. _____

3. _____

4. _____

Your role as a maker of sunrise experiences for those you meet on your voyage can bring personal happiness for yourself as well as those you touch. Familiarity with geography, places, and people can be heartwarming and contribute to your sense of well-being.

Your well-being can also receive a boost from even a small amount of attention to your appearance. No, you're not going to be thirty again, but you'd be amazed how much your attitude can improve when you look in the mirror and like what you see. Maintaining a youthful and professional appearance supports your sense of self-worth. And no, you're not being vain.

So keep your wardrobe current, get regular exercise, buy a smartphone, and visit a country you have always wanted to experience. Any of these alone can make you feel better, and all of them together will change your level of optimism entirely. That's the most important part.

Optimism is a key element of the afterlife. Work hard at becoming less quarrelsome and more patient. Be kinder and more understanding. Stay positive. Stay involved and connected with the world at large; don't isolate yourself. You have earned a great after-life. Now enjoy it to the fullest.

Even though these lessons have reached their full level of importance for me only recently, I learned them when I was young. I was born during the Great Depression—nowadays we might call it the Very Great Recession, but those were simpler times.

My family experienced the Great Depression first-hand in a small town in Pennsylvania, where barter and sharing were the keys to survival after the town's principal employer, a rayon plant, closed. We were fortunate because we had an orchard and large veg-etable garden behind our house, and our food cellar was filled with mason jars of apples, peaches, cherries, squash, and tomatoes. Those fruits and vegetables, along with a few chickens from our chicken coop, sustained us during some very hard times.

My mother gave us spiritual nourishment, too. Her kindness was legendary, and we all learned the wisdom of living generously by watching her. We had a flow of travelers or hoboes, who would knock on our back door looking for something to eat. My mother always found something nutritious—along with a piece of pie—and sent them on their way with smiles on their faces. She was always careful to preserve their dignity, too, by finding small chores for them to do so they felt they earned the meal.

My mother made it very clear to me that I had a responsibility to others and that my goal in life was to leave this earth better than I found it. Though she lived through the Great Depression, she was always an optimist who found something good in most situations. Her glass was always half full, and her five children adopted this wonderful, positive attitude.

Extending a helping hand to those less fortunate is an important part of achieving an inner peace as our senior lives unfold. If we truly want to leave the world a better place, then our senior years should not be wasted with inactivity and lack of involvement with others. We should remain or become a proactive force for good in our communities. Inner peace will surely follow.

Evolution

Time has carried us across many oceans
Exploring new continents, marching to
The beat of an often distant drummer
A journey of discovery through
Valleys of relentless, demanding change
The years tumbling one upon another
With you the only constant
Watching time have its way with me
Silently accepting as I evolve
From one person to another
Covering me with a warm blanket
Of unconditional love, always
Celebrating both who I was and
Who I might yet be

Robert John Emmons
exploring a country road